SCIENCE FAIR PROJECTS

Astronomy and Space

Kelly Milner Halls

Heinemann Library
Chicago, Illinois

Customer Service 888-454-2279
Visit our website at www.heinemannlibrary.com

Designed by Kimberly R. Miracle and Fiona MacColl
Illustrations by Cavedweller Studios
Printed in China by Leo Paper Group

11 10 09
10 9 8 7 6 5 4 3 2

ISBNs: ISBN-13: 978-1-4034-7908-2 (hc) : ISBN-10: 1-4034-7908-9 (hc)

Library of Congress Cataloging-in-Publication Data
Halls, Kelly Milner, 1957-
  Astronomy and space / Kelly Milner Halls.
    p. cm. -- (Science fair projects)
  Includes bibliographical references and index.
  ISBN-13: 978-1-4034-7908-2 (hardcover) 1. Science projects--Juvenile literature. 2.
Astronomy projects--Juvenile literature. 3. Astronomy--Juvenile literature. 4. Outer space--
Juvenile literature. I. Title.
  Q182.3.H35 2007
  520.78--dc22
                              2006025458

Acknowledgments
The author and publishers are grateful to the following for permission to reproduce copyright
material: Bridgeman Art Library, **p. 38**; Corbis RF, **p. 20**; Corbis/Sanford/Agliolo, **p. 28**; Getty
Images/Image Bank, **p. 24**; Getty Images/Photodisc, **pp. 13, 16, 31**; Ifa-Bilderteam Gmbh/OSF,
p. 12; Masterfile/ Andrew Douglas, **p. 4**; NASA, **pp. 6** (JPL-Caltech), **36**; Science Photo Library,
pp. 8 (Mark Garlick), **26** (Ian Steele & Ian Hutcheon), **32** (Detlev Van Ravenswaay), **p. 40** (Pekka
Parviainen), **14** (The Kobal Collection/Hammer).

Cover photograph reproduced with permission of Getty Images/Photodisc. Background
illustration by istockphoto.com.

Every effort has been made to contact copyright holders of any material reproduced
in this book. Any omissions will be rectified in subsequent printings if notice is given
to the publisher.

» Some words are shown in bold, **like this**. You can
find the definitions for these words in the glossary.

Contents

Science Fair Basics

Starting a science fair project can be an exciting challenge. You can test **scientific theory** by developing an appropriate scientific question. Then you can search, using the thoughtful steps of a well-planned experiment, for the answer to that question. It's like a treasure hunt of the mind.

In a way, your mission is to better understand how your world and the things in it work. You may be rewarded with a good grade or an award for your scientific hard work. But no matter what scores your project receives, you'll be a winner. That's because you will know a little bit more about your subject than you did before you started.

In this book, we'll look at nine different science fair projects related to space and astronomy. We will discover amazing things about Earth and beyond.

Do Your Research

Is there something about astronomy and space you've always wondered about? Something you don't quite understand but would like to? Then do a little research about the subject. Go to the library and check out books about the subject that interests you.

Use your favorite Internet search engine to find reliable online sources. Museums, universities, scientific journals, newspapers, and magazines are among the best sources for accurate research. Each experiment in this book lists some suggestions for further research.

When doing research you need to make sure your sources are reliable. Ask yourself the following questions about sources, especially those you find online.

The Experiments

The beginning of each experiment contains a box like this.

Possible Question:

This question is a suggested starting point for your experiment. You will need to adapt the question to reflect your own interests.

Possible Hypothesis:

Don't worry if your hypothesis doesn't match the one listed here, this is only a suggestion.

Approximate Cost of Materials:

Discuss this with your parents before beginning work.

Materials Needed:

Make sure you can easily get all of the materials listed and gather them before beginning work.

Level of Difficulty:

There are three levels of experiments in this book: Easy, Intermediate, and Hard. The level of difficulty is based on how long the experiment takes and how complicated it is.

1) How old is the source? Is it possible that the information is outdated?

2) Who wrote the source? Is there an identifiable author, and is the author qualified to write about the topic?

3) What is the purpose of the source? The website of a telescope company may not be the best place to find out how strong a telescope you should buy.

4) Is the information well documented? Can you tell where the author got his or her information?

Some websites allow you to "chat" online with experts. Make sure you discuss this with your parent or teacher before participating. Never give out private information, including your address, online.

Once you know a little more about the subject you want to explore, you'll be ready to ask a science project question and form an intelligent **hypothesis**. A hypothesis is an educated guess about what the results of your experiment will be. Finally, you'll be ready to begin your science fair exploration!

Continued →

What Is an Experiment?

When you say you're going to "experiment" you may just mean that you're going to try something out. When a scientist uses that word though, he or she means something else. In a proper experiment you have **variables** and a **control**. A variable is something that changes. The independent variable is the thing you purposely change as part of the experiment. The dependent variable is the change that happens in response to the thing you do. The controlled variables, or control group, are the things you do not change so that you have something to compare your outcomes to. Here's an example: Ten people have headaches. You give 5 people (Group A) asprins. You do not allow 5 people (Group B) to do anything for their headaches. Group A is the independent variable. The effects of the asprins are the dependent variable. Group B is a control group. To make sure the experiment is accurate though, you need to do it several times.

Some of the projects in this book are not proper experiments. They are projects designed to help you learn about a subject. You need to check with your teacher about whether these projects are appropriate for your science fair. Make sure you know all the science fair rules about what kinds of projects and materials are allowed before beginning.

What would be the best way to explore these stars?

Your Hypothesis

Once you've decided what question you're going to try to answer, you'll want to make a scientific **prediction** of what you'll discover through your science project. For example, if you wonder how it feels to be an astronaut on a long mission your question might be "How does gravity affect sleep?"

Remember, a hypothesis is an educated guess about how your experiment will turn out—what results you'll observe. So your hypothesis in response to the above question might be, "Living in zero gravity makes it hard to sleep." The hypothesis is your best guess of how things might turn out when the experiment has been completed. It's also a good way to find out if you can actually complete the steps needed to answer your project question. If your question is, "How many stars are there in the sky?," it will be impossible to prove your hypothesis, no matter what you make it. So, be sure the evidence to prove or disprove your hypothesis is actually within reach.

Research Journal

It is very important to keep careful notes about your project. From start to finish, make entries in your research journal so you won't have to rely on memory when it comes time to create your display. What time did you start your experiment? How long did you work on it each day? What were the variables, or things that changed, about your experimental setting? How did they change and why? What things did you overlook in planning your project? How did you solve the problems, once you discovered them?

These are the kinds of questions you'll answer in your research journal. No detail is too small when it comes to scientific research. You'll find some tips on writing your report and preparing a great display at the back of this book on pages 44–46. Use these and the tips in each project as guides, but don't be afraid to get creative. Make your display, and your project, your own.

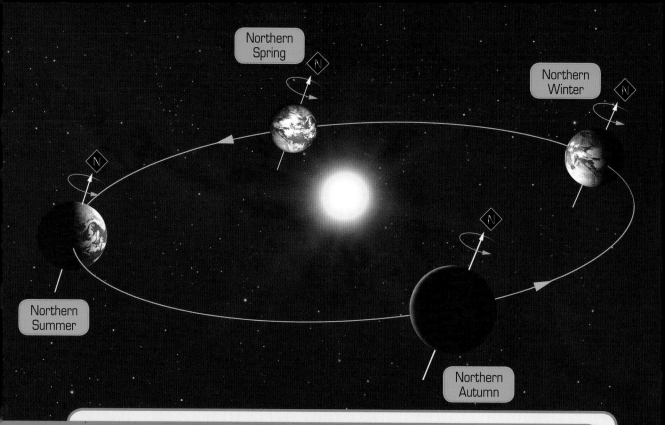

Northern
Spring

Northern
Winter

Northern
Summer

Northern
Autumn

Here Comes the Sun

In North America, summer days are longer than winter days. The position of Earth changes in relation to the Sun, so the Sun doesn't seem to sink into the horizon until much later in the day. In the winter it sets earlier, so the days are shorter. But have you ever noticed Earth's position change with each passing day? You will now.

Do Your Research

This project deals with the astronomical situation that causes the different seasons and changing length of days we experience on Earth. Before you begin your project, do some research to find out more about Earth's **orbit** and relationship with the Sun. Once you've done some research, you can tackle this project. Or, you may come up with your own unique project after you've read and learned more about the topic.

Here are some books and websites you could start with in your research:

» Asimov, Isaac and Richard Hantula. *The Sun.* Milwaukee: Gareth Stevens, 2003.
» Pipe, Jim. *The Sun.* Mankato, MN: Stargazer Books, 2004.

Continued

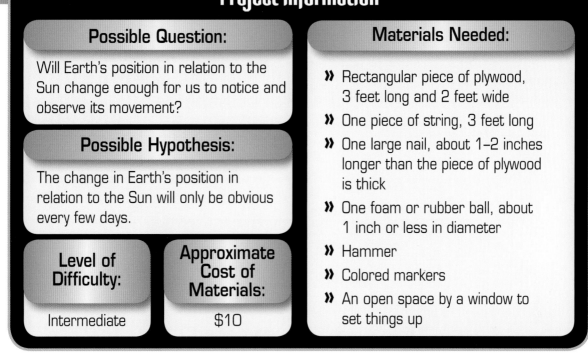

Project Information

Possible Question:

Will Earth's position in relation to the Sun change enough for us to notice and observe its movement?

Possible Hypothesis:

The change in Earth's position in relation to the Sun will only be obvious every few days.

Level of Difficulty:

Intermediate

Approximate Cost of Materials:

$10

Materials Needed:

» Rectangular piece of plywood, 3 feet long and 2 feet wide
» One piece of string, 3 feet long
» One large nail, about 1–2 inches longer than the piece of plywood is thick
» One foam or rubber ball, about 1 inch or less in diameter
» Hammer
» Colored markers
» An open space by a window to set things up

» The Farmer's Almanac: http://www.farmersalmanac.com/astronomy/astronomy.html
» Here Comes the Sun: http://www.vortex.plymouth.edu/sun/sunl.html
» Solar Views: http://www.solarviews.com/eng/sun.htm

Steps to Success:

1. Using a ruler, find the exact center of the rectangle of wood and draw a line across it, as if you were going to cut the piece of wood in half.

2. Mark a spot on that center line about 1/4 inch from the edge of the wood.

3. Place the wood on a stable surface you and your family don't care much about. This is important, because that surface may be damaged in the next step.

Continued →

Step 5

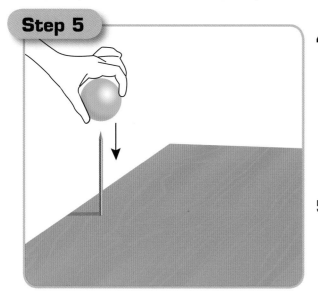

Step 8

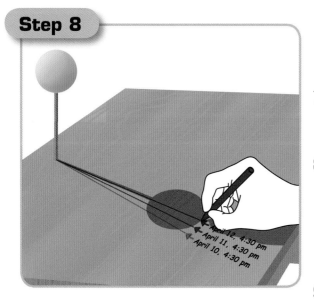

April 12, 4:30 pm
April 11, 4:30 pm
April 10, 4:30 pm

4. Hammer your nail all the way through the spot you marked near the edge of the wood.

The head of the nail should be flush with the top of the board, and the tip of the nail should come through and stick out of the bottom.

5. Carefully turn the wood over, watching for the tip of the nail that you pounded through. Push the foam or rubber ball onto the sharp point of the nail to protect yourself from puncture wounds.

6. Place the board, with the tip of the nail up, on a spot near a window where the afternoon sun directly shines in. This should be a spot where it can stay, unmoved, for a whole month.

7. At the same time every day, observe the shadow the nail casts on the board as the Sun shines in the window.

8. Mark the shadow on the board with a colored marker and date it. You'll be making many records like this, so try not to take up too much space on the board. Duplicate this record in your research journal as well.

9. Repeat steps 7 and 8 every day at the same time for one month.

Result Summary:

» Did the shadow move each day?

» Through the month, could you tell just by looking out the window that the Earth had moved enough to change the Sun's position in the sky?

Added Activities to Give Your Project Extra Punch:

» Check the shadows twice a day.

» Do the same experiment at a set time each night, using moonlight.

Display Extras:

» A collection of images depicting the Sun, accurately and artistically.

» A spotlight shining on your board and nail to mimic the shadow you originally observed.

» Two Styrofoam balls representing the Earth and the Sun. You could draw the rough continental details on the ball representing Earth and use a pushpin to indicate the location of your hometown in North America. Then you could give the Earth the proper tilt (based on your research) to show how the sunlight would hit our planet during a specific season of the year.

Mooning Around

Have you ever looked at the Moon's phases — how it seems to change from a circle to a thin sliver in the course of a month? Do those changes impact life on Earth? This project might help you decide.

Do Your Research

This project takes one month to complete. The project deals with the phases of the Moon and how the Moon might affect you during its cycle. Before you begin your project, do some research to find out more about the Moon's phases. You will also want to research popular ideas about the Moon and how it affects people. Once you've done some research, you can tackle this project. Or, you may come up with your own unique project after you've read and learned more about the topic.

Here are some books and websites you could start with in your research:

» Knocke, Melanie Melton. *From Blue Moons to Black Holes: A Basic Guide to Astronomy, Outer Space, and Space Exploration.* Amherst, NY: Prometheus Books, 2005.

» NASA: the Moon:
http://nssdc.gsfc.nasa.gov/planetary/planets/moonpage.html

» Virtual Reality: The Moon's Phases: http://tycho.usno.navy.mil/vphase.html

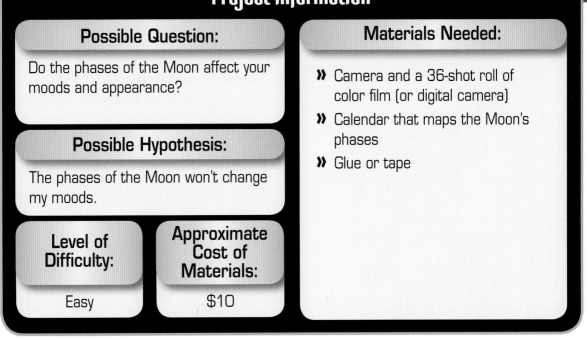

Project Information

Possible Question:

Do the phases of the Moon affect your moods and appearance?

Possible Hypothesis:

The phases of the Moon won't change my moods.

Level of Difficulty:

Easy

Approximate Cost of Materials:

$10

Materials Needed:

» Camera and a 36-shot roll of color film (or digital camera)
» Calendar that maps the Moon's phases
» Glue or tape

Steps to Success:

1. Before you start the project, copy each phase of the Moon into your research journal. Use a new page of your journal for each phase. Make sure to start the project with whatever phase is first in your journal.

2. Be sure to go to bed and wake up at the same time each day for the duration of your project.

3. At the same time each day in the morning, afternoon, and evening, make a note about your mood and record each observation in your research journal. Note if you are happy, sad, or average each day, three times a day.

The Moon

Continued →

There are many stories about what happens at a full Moon. Watch your moods carefully.

4. Observe your general appearance at the same time each morning and take notes. Record these details in your research journal along with the date and time. Is your complexion pale? Is your hair shiny? Is your breath fresh or stale? Is your skin dry or moisturized?

5. Have someone take a picture of you after you've made your notes each morning as a record of your observations.

6. Each evening at sunset, sketch your own version of the phase of the Moon, to compare to the sketches of the Moon's phases you previously copied from a science book. If the Moon is not visible, refer to your calendar, copy the Moon's phase, and record these steps in your research journal.

7. At the end of the month, process the film and glue or tape each photo onto the coordinating page of your research journal.

Result Summary:

» Did you notice any trends in your moods?

» Did they change when the Moon's phases changed?

» Did your complexion change at all during the Moon's cycle?

» Did the shine of your hair change?

» Did your skin get dry or stay the same during different phases?

» Were there other factors involved that might have affected your results on certain days?

Added Activities to Give Your Project Extra Punch:

» Chart the number of days each phase of the Moon lasted.

» Chart your daily moods, using a hand-drawn or sticker symbol for each category — happy, sad, average.

» Draw a chart of the phases of the Moon and pick one picture of you to illustrate your mood and appearance during that phase.

» Ask someone to keep notes on your daily moods, separate from your own notes. See if those notes match your own.

» Get your friends or siblings to chart their moods and compare the results.

» If you have time, repeat the experiment for another month and see if your observations stayed the same or changed.

Display Extras:

» Model of the Moon

» Images representing people in different moods

» Information about different myths or stories that involve the Moon and mood changes, such as stories about full Moons.

Count on It

Many people love stargazing But how have modern life and technology changed what we see in the night sky? This project will shed some "light" on the subject.

Do Your Research

This project deals with the observable night sky and how artificial light affects the view. Before you begin your project, do some research to find out more about the night sky, the stars and other objects that are visible to the bare eye, and what "light pollution" is. Once you've done some research, you can tackle this project. Or, you may come up with your own unique project after you've read and learned more about the topic.

Here are some books and websites you could start with in your research:

» Harrington, Philip S. *Star Watch: The Amateur Astronomer's Guide to Finding, Observing, and Learning about More Than 125 Celestial Objects.* Hoboken, NJ: John Wiley & Sons, 2003.

» Stargazing Basics: http://www.skytonight.com/howto/basics/

» Be a Stargazer: http://www.pbs.org/wgbh/nova/worlds/stargazer.html

» Star Date Online: http://stardate.org/nightsky/

Project Information

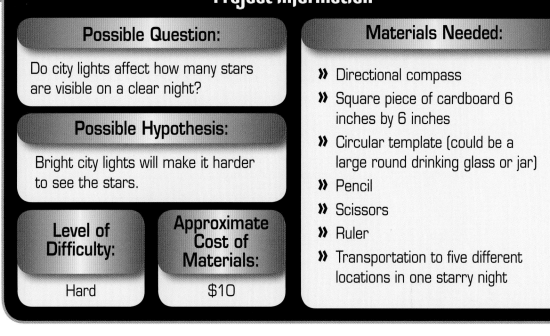

Possible Question:

Do city lights affect how many stars are visible on a clear night?

Possible Hypothesis:

Bright city lights will make it harder to see the stars.

Level of Difficulty:

Hard

Approximate Cost of Materials:

$10

Materials Needed:

» Directional compass
» Square piece of cardboard 6 inches by 6 inches
» Circular template (could be a large round drinking glass or jar)
» Pencil
» Scissors
» Ruler
» Transportation to five different locations in one starry night

Steps to Success:

1. Using your circular template (such as a glass or jar), trace a circle close to the center on your square of cardboard.

2. Cut the circle out of the cardboard.

3. Select five locations, from very brightly lit, like a chain store parking lot, to dimly lit, like a natural park.

4. Wait for a clear night, with few or no clouds.

5. Record the time you set out and visit each of the five locations as quickly as possible, so that the night sky will not have changed much in between each location. Also record the time you arrive at each location. Be sure to have a trusted adult with you anytime you do a project outside at night.

ADULT SUPERVISION REQUIRED

Continued ➔

6. Choose a specific star from a **constellation** you know and will recognize, such as the Big Dipper. Hold the cardboard circle six inches from your eyes, using a ruler to be as accurate as possible each time. Look through the hole and make sure the star you chose is as close to the exact center as possible each time.

7. Count the stars you can see inside that defined circle.

8. Record the time, location, and star count in your research journal.

9. Move to each of the other four locations and repeat steps 6, 7, and 8 each time.

10. Repeat the same steps on a second, clear night, starting at the same time and reversing the order in which you visit the locations. This will help you to know how the changes in time could affect star visibility.

Result Summary:

» Did the number of stars you counted remain the same or change with light levels?

» How great were the changes, if there were any?

» Did the passing of time also affect the number of stars you were able to see?

Added Activities to Give Your Project Extra Punch:

» Chart the star totals, locations, and times to visually compare them.

» Ask your parent or guardian to repeat the experiment standing back-to-back with you and compare the results.

» Repeat the experiment several times and take an average of the star counts.

» Repeat the experiment on a more cloudy evening and compare.

» Repeat the experiment on a night with a full Moon, then on a night with no Moon.

» Repeat the experiment on a windy evening and compare.

Display Extras:

» Hang each number of stars from a wire coat hanger so people can compare the "look" of the numbers, rather than the figures alone. In other words, 30 stars have a greater visual impact in the dark of night than 4 stars in the glare of city lights.

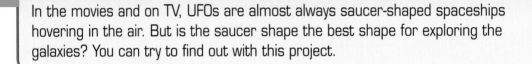

Staying in [Space] Shape

In the movies and on TV, UFOs are almost always saucer-shaped spaceships hovering in the air. But is the saucer shape the best shape for exploring the galaxies? You can try to find out with this project.

Do Your Research

This project deals with how shape might affect the ability of objects to fly in our sky. Before you begin your project, do some research to find out more about objects that fly in our sky and in space and the shapes they take. Find out why they were designed with their particular shapes. You can also take a look at UFO evidence and observe the shapes of the objects that have supposedly been seen. Make note of those shapes and why they might make sense if these vehicles existed. Once you've done some research, you can tackle this project. Or, you may come up with your own unique project after you've read and learned more about the topic.

Here are some books and websites you could start with in your research:

» Parker, Steve. *The Science of Air: Projects and Experiments on Air and Flight.* Chicago: Heinemann Library, 2005.

» Wallace, Lane E. *Wild Blue Wonders: Exploring the Magic of Flight.* Oshkosh, WI.: EAA (Experimental Aircraft Association), 2001.

» Space Craft: http://www.yahooligans.yahoo.com/content/science/space/spacecraft.html

» World Almanac for Kids: http://www.worldalmanacforkids.com/explore/space/spacecraft.html

Project Information

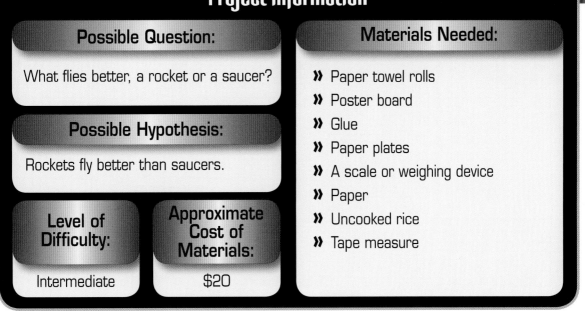

Possible Question:

What flies better, a rocket or a saucer?

Possible Hypothesis:

Rockets fly better than saucers.

Level of Difficulty:

Intermediate

Approximate Cost of Materials:

$20

Materials Needed:

» Paper towel rolls
» Poster board
» Glue
» Paper plates
» A scale or weighing device
» Paper
» Uncooked rice
» Tape measure

Steps to Success:

1. Using a paper towel roll and poster board, build a simple rocket-shaped device leaving the end open.

Step 1

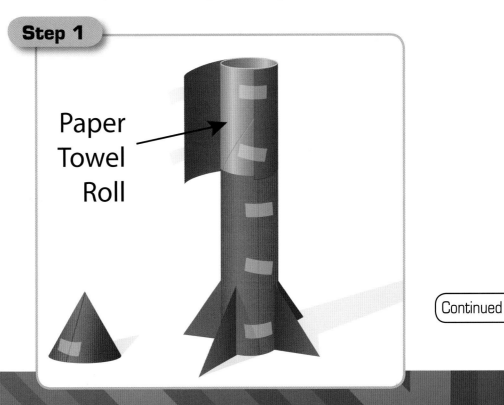

Paper Towel Roll

Continued ⊕

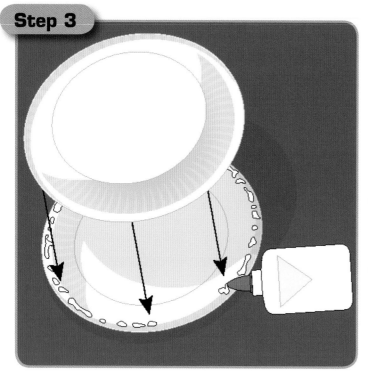

2. Weigh the device once it is completed.

3. Glue two paper plates together to create a flying saucer-shaped object, leaving a two-inch section open on one side.

4. Pour grains of uncooked rice into each flying object until their weights are equal.

5. Seal the openings on the rocket and the saucer with tape exactly the same length so that the weights remain equal and the rice cannot escape the objects.

6. Mark a starting point and launch both objects using the same method. Try to be careful to apply the same force to your manual launch with each object, so your starts will be nearly identical.

7. Measure how far each model flew, using a tape measure from your launch point to your landing location. Be careful to measure accurately and to record your data in your research journal.

8. Repeat steps 6 and 7 five more times for each object and record the results.

9. Take an average of the distances each object traveled in order to reduce the effect of human error on the accuracy of your experiment.

10. Chart the compared results.

Result Summary:

» Did both models perform equally?

» Did both seem to fly with equal ease?

» Why did one fly better than the other, if one did?

» What would you do to change the results?

Added Activities to Give Your Project Extra Punch:

» Research real space vehicles and their shapes and compare them to your models.

» Examine alleged UFO photographs and chart how many looked like a saucer and how many looked like a rocket.

» Repeat the experiment when it is windy and calm. Record the differences.

» Explain why both rockets and saucers are needed to explore space.

Display Extras:

» UFO and alien toys and spacecraft and rocket models could be fun for this display.

Catch a Falling Star

Have you ever seen a falling star? "Falling stars" are actually tiny bits of space rock or **meteorites** pulled into the Earth's **atmosphere** by gravity. They glow and spark with heat as they fall through the atmosphere, and we see the shimmer. But are all meteorites big enough for us to see them falling? Try this project to find out.

Do Your Research

This project deals with meteorites and space particles that make their way to the earth's surface. Before you begin your project, do some research to find out more about meteorites. Once you've done some research, you can tackle this project. Or, you may come up with your own unique project after you've read and learned more about the topic.

Here are some books and websites you could start with in your research:

» Miller, Ron. *Asteroids, Comets, and Meteors.* Minneapolis, MN: Lerner Publishing, 2004.

» Reynolds, Michael D. *Falling Stars: A Guide to Meteors and Meteorites.* Minneapolis, MN.: Sagebrush, 2003.

» The American Meteor Society: http://www.amsmeteors.org

» Asteroids: Deadly Impact: http://www.nationalgeographic.com/asteroids/

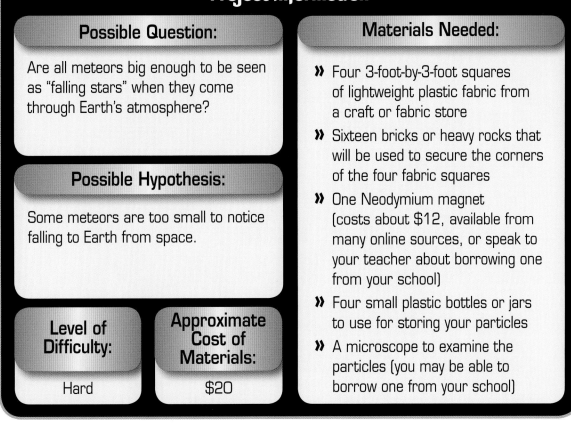

Project Information

Possible Question:

Are all meteors big enough to be seen as "falling stars" when they come through Earth's atmosphere?

Possible Hypothesis:

Some meteors are too small to notice falling to Earth from space.

Level of Difficulty:

Hard

Approximate Cost of Materials:

$20

Materials Needed:

» Four 3-foot-by-3-foot squares of lightweight plastic fabric from a craft or fabric store

» Sixteen bricks or heavy rocks that will be used to secure the corners of the four fabric squares

» One Neodymium magnet (costs about $12, available from many online sources, or speak to your teacher about borrowing one from your school)

» Four small plastic bottles or jars to use for storing your particles

» A microscope to examine the particles (you may be able to borrow one from your school)

Steps to Success:

1. On a dry, sunny, still day, set your four plastic fabric squares in an open outdoor area.

2. Use bricks or rocks on each corner of each square to keep them grounded and level.

3. After two hours, very carefully gather the corners of the first fabric square and pull them up to get anything that gathered on the fabric to fall to the center.

4. Gently tap the sides of the gathered fabric to get the remaining particles to fall to the center.

5. Place your magnet under the fabric directly under the little heap of dust that was collected and blow very gently.

Continued →

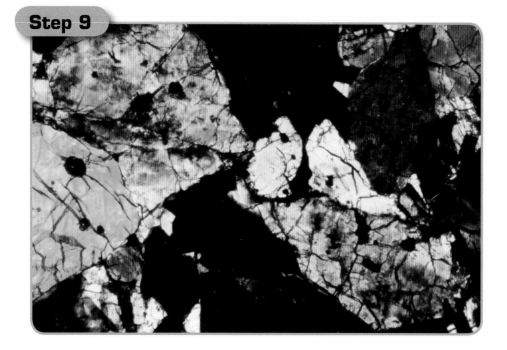

6. Make a note in your research journal about what blew away.

7. Gather what sticks to the magnet into a small collection jar or bottle.

8. Repeat steps 3, 4, 5, 6, and 7 with each square.

9. Examine your collected particles under a microscope to see if they are meteoric. Compare your particles to photos of meteorites you found in your research.

10. If possible, set up an appointment with a **geologist** to look at your findings. You may be able to find a geology professor at your local college. There may also be a United States Geological Survey Office in your area. This step is optional, but if you want to include it, make sure to plan ahead so that you have enough time to set up an interview.

Result Summary:

» What was caught on the plastic fabric most often?

» How did you confirm that some particles were micrometeors?

Added Activities to Give Your Project Extra Punch:

» Weigh your particles and estimate how many it would take to make a small meteor you can hold in your hand.

» Research how many different kinds of meteors there are.

» Find out how many particles in everyday dirt are actually space particles.

» Find out what shape most micrometeors are once they strike Earth.

Display Extras:

» Display some of the particles you caught under a microscope, and some loose in a collection jar.

» Display the magnet you used.

WHAM! BAM! CRASH!

As we previously learned, meteors and meteorites hit Earth on a fairly regular basis. There are some famous craters such as Meteor Crater in Arizona, but usually weathering and **erosion** make the craters hard to recognize. However, life on the Moon is different. Craters on the Moon are numerous and visible. The piles of rock around a crater are known as **ejecta**. The bright streaks of material that shoot out are known as rays. In this project you'll look at factors that affect what the ejecta and rays look like.

Do Your Research

This project looks at how the size of an object crashing into the moon might affect the appearance of the crater, the ejecta, and the rays. Before you begin your project do some research into the moon's surface, meteors, and impact craters. Once you've done your research you can crash into this project. Or, you may want to come up with your own unique project after you've read about the topic.

Here are some books and websites you could start with in your research:

» Chaisson, Eric and Steve McMillan. *Astronomy Today.* Old Tappan, NJ: Prentice Hall, 2002.

» Gardner, Robert. *Planet Earth Science Fair Projects.* Berkeley Heights, NJ: Enslow, 2005.

» Craters of the Moon National Monument: http://nps.gov/crmo/pphtml/forkids.html

» Lunar and Planetary Instititue: http://www.lpi.usra.edu

Project Information

Possible Question:

Does the size of an object affect the appearance of a crater?

Possible Hypothesis:

Larger objects will create larger and more interesting looking craters.

Level of Difficulty:

Intermediate

Approximate Cost of Materials:

$10

Materials Needed:

» 1 jawbreaker or other hard candy
» 1 marble
» 1 orange or other non-bouncing round object of this size
» Large aluminum roasting pan or cardboard box
» Any of the following: flour, play sand, corn meal, or baking powder (enough to fill the pan 3 to 5 inches high several times)
» Tempera paints or instant hot chocolate mix or other colored, powdered drink mix (note: real cocoa does not work as well)
» Newspaper or plastic sheet to place under the pan
» Ruler
» Protractor
» Camera and film or digital camera (optional)

Steps to Success:

1. In your research journal create three charts similar to the one shown. Use these charts to record your results in steps 6 and 7.

Step 1

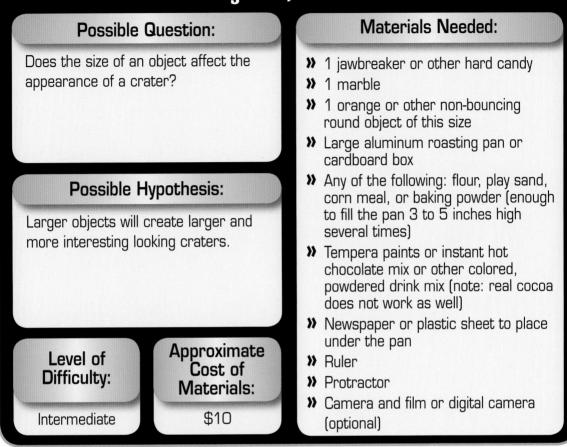

Object 1: Jawbreaker

	1st Trial	2nd Trial	3rd Trial	Average
Crater Diameter				
Crater Depth				
Average Length of Rays				

Continued →

2. Place the newspaper or plastic under the pan.

3. Fill the pan with 3 to 5 inches of flour.

4. Sprinkle a light coating of the paint or colored powder over the flour, this will help make any changes more visible.

5. Stand on the floor, hold the jawbreaker at shoulder height, and drop it into the pan.

6. Use your ruler to measure the depth and length of the rays.

7. Use your protractor to measure the diameter.

8. You may wish to take a picture of your crater.

9. Empty and refill the pan, or smooth out the flour and repeat steps 5–8 two more times. Make sure you drop the jawbreaker from the same height each time.

10. Empty and refill the pan, or smooth out the flour and repeat steps 1–9 with the marble and then the orange. You may wish to use a different color of tempera paint for each object to make it easier to remember which photos belong to which objects. Make sure to keep the height you drop the objects from consistent.

11. Graph or chart the data you've collected.

12. Mount the best of your pictures on your display.

Result Summary:

» What effect did the size of the object have on the diameter of the crater?

» What effect did the size of the object have on the depth of the crater?

» What effect did the size of the object have on the length of the rays?

» Based on your research, what are the reasons we see more craters on the Moon than on Earth?

Added Activities to Give Your Project Extra Punch:

» Repeat the experiment, only this time drop the balls from different heights. How does this affect the craters?

» Repet the experiment, only this time try to drop the balls at an angle. How does this affect the craters?

Display Extras:

» Have materials available for people to create their own craters. (Make sure to discuss this idea with your teacher first as this could be considered too messy.)

» Display your "meteors."

» Display photos of Moon and Earth craters

» Collect and display photographs of famous impact craters on Earth.

» Collect and display photographs of impact craters on the Moon and other planets.

How big was the object that created this crater?

Total Eclipse

Pictures of lunar or solar **eclipses** look amazing — almost too amazing to believe. Is it really possible for planets, moons, and stars to align to create this vision? Two balls and a flashlight can help you find out.

Do Your Research

This project deals with the astronomical movements and situations that create solar and lunar eclipses. Before you begin your project, do some research to find out more about eclipses and the movements of Earth and its Moon. Once you've done some research, you can tackle this project. Or, you may come up with your own unique project after you've read and learned more about the topic.

Here are some books and websites you could start with in your research:

» Asimov, Isaac and Richard Hantula. *The Sun*. Milwaukee: Gareth Stevens, 2003.

» Cole, Michael D. *The Sun: The Center of the Solar System*. Berkeley Heights, NJ: Enslow, 2001.

» Mr. Eclipse: http://www.mreclipse.com

» NASA's Eclipse Homepage: http://sunearth.gsfc.nasa.gov/eclipse/eclipse.html

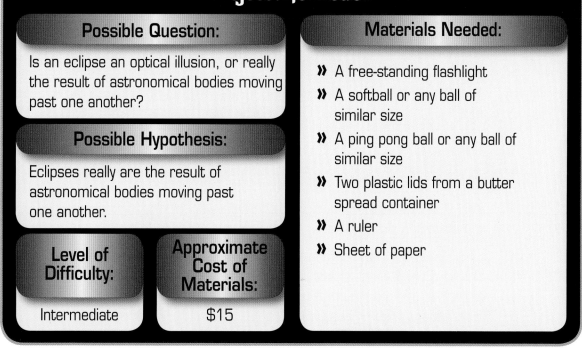

Project Information

Possible Question:

Is an eclipse an optical illusion, or really the result of astronomical bodies moving past one another?

Possible Hypothesis:

Eclipses really are the result of astronomical bodies moving past one another.

Level of Difficulty:

Intermediate

Approximate Cost of Materials:

$15

Materials Needed:

» A free-standing flashlight
» A softball or any ball of similar size
» A ping pong ball or any ball of similar size
» Two plastic lids from a butter spread container
» A ruler
» Sheet of paper

Steps to Success:

1. Place the softball, or whatever larger ball you are using, on a piece of paper on a large, flat surface. Put a plastic lid beneath the ball to prevent it from rolling. This will be your **stationary**, or unmoving, ball. Be sure there is a blank wall behind so you can see its shadow when light is shined on it from the front.

2. Draw a circle with an 8-inch **radius** around the larger ball. This means the distance from the center of the ball to any point on the circle should be 8 inches. This will be the orbit for the ping pong, or smaller, ball.

3. Place the ping pong ball, or whatever smaller ball you are using, on the circle directly to the right of the larger ball, also on a plastic lid to keep it from rolling.

4. Turn on the flashlight and set it in line with the larger ball, so you can see its shadow on the wall.

Continued ⊕

Step 5

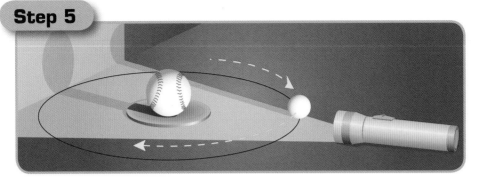

5. Now slowly move the smaller, orbiting ball along its orbit (the circle) in a clockwise direction.

6. As the balls begin to line up, or intersect the shadow, stop the movement in at least six places to observe the shadow on the larger ball and the shadows on the wall. Draw and record your observations in your research journal at each stop. Be sure to number the drawings and observations you make in order to remember the sequence.

7. Repeat this process until the balls line up exactly, one in front of the other, with the light beam of the flashlight. Make careful sketches of what you see in your research journal.

8. Continue to move the smaller ball on its orbit (the circle) around the larger ball, again stopping at several places to record your observations, until the smaller ball is once again in the place where it started its orbit, directly to the right of the larger ball.

Step 8

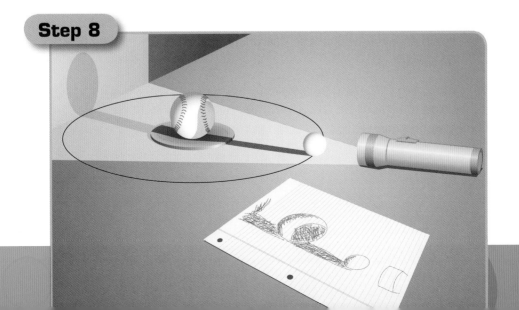

Result Summary:

» How did the shadows change as the balls came together in a line, and then apart?
» What impact did the flashlight have on both shadows?
» How does this simulate an eclipse of the Sun or the Moon?

Added Activities to Give Your Project Extra Punch:

» Repeat the process with the flashlight between the balls and record the patterns in your research journal.
» Repeat the experiment with the flashlight behind the balls, and see if the results change.

Display Extras:

» Display the props used for your illustrated presentation board.
» Display a small model of the solar system's obits, or at least the orbits of the Earth and its Moon around the Sun.
» Display photos of solar and lunar eclipses.

Twinkle, Twinkle Little Star

When we see glitter, or the reflection of light on a diamond, we are perhaps reminded of the twinkle of starlight. But do stars really twinkle? And if they do, when do they twinkle most?

Do Your Research

This project deals with how we see the light of a star from the surface of Earth. Before you begin your project, do some research to find out more about how the light from stars travels to Earth, and how our atmosphere might affect what we see. Once you've done some research, you can tackle this project. Or, you may come up with your own unique project after you've read and learned more about the topic.

Here are some books and websites you could start with in your research:

» Brunier, Serge. *The Concise Atlas of Stars*. New York: Firefly Books, 2005.

» Chaisson, Eric and Steve McMillan. *Astronomy Today*. Upper Saddle River, NJ: Prentice Hall, 2002.

» Farmer's Almanac: http://www.farmersalmanac.com/astronomy/astronomy.html

» Stars: University of Illinois: http://www.astro.uiuc.edu/~kaler/sow/sowlist.html

Project Information

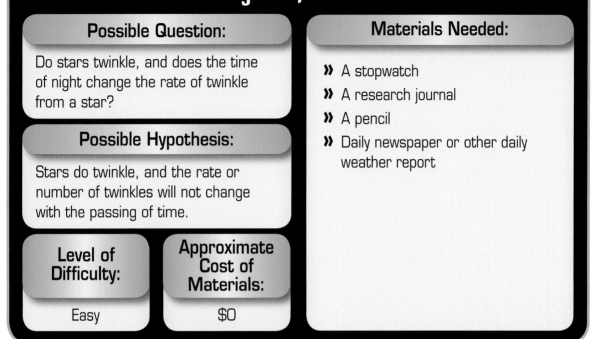

Possible Question:

Do stars twinkle, and does the time of night change the rate of twinkle from a star?

Possible Hypothesis:

Stars do twinkle, and the rate or number of twinkles will not change with the passing of time.

Level of Difficulty:

Easy

Approximate Cost of Materials:

$0

Materials Needed:

» A stopwatch
» A research journal
» A pencil
» Daily newspaper or other daily weather report

Steps to Success:

1. Record the day's weather and make a note of your start time in your research journal.

2. Pick an easily identifiable (and easily traceable) star to observe.

3. Every five minutes, set the stopwatch to ten seconds, start it, and count the "twinkles," or visual blinks, of your star during that ten seconds. Make a note of the number of twinkles you observed in your research journal. If possible, have an assistant work the stopwatch for you.

4. Repeat the process every five minutes for an hour.

5. Graph the data (number of twinkles observed) you gathered in your research journal.

Continued →

6. Repeat steps 1–5 on other nights, and try to get as much variation in weather as possible.

7. Analyze the data to determine if the rate of the twinkle of the star changes in any given night, or if it changes with different weather conditions.

Vincent Van Gogh's famous painting "Starry Night" is just one example of how the twinkling of stars has inspired people.

Result Summary:

» Did the number of twinkles stay the same, increase, or decrease as time passed?

» Did the intensity of the twinkle remain constant?

» Did changes in the weather — wind, fog, clouds — affect your observations?

Added Activities to Give Your Project Extra Punch:

» Try observing a different star to see if all stars behave the same.

» Try observing the star over a longer period of time and see if there is a change in the rate of its twinkle.

» On another night, repeat a similar, briefer observation experiment, looking for changes in star twinkle color.

» On another night, try to observe a planet rather than a star and see if it twinkles.

Display Extras:

» Glitter might be especially effective in your project display.

» Holiday lights might also enhance the impact of your project.

finding a Heavenly Body

For centuries, seafaring travelers used the stars in the sky to be sure they were headed in the right direction. As they gazed at the seemingly unchanging stars in the night sky, they also imagined pictures we came to call constellations: Orion the archer, Leo the lion, Pegasus the flying steed. Are these constellations all equally visible?

Do Your Research

This project deals with constellations in the night sky. You may need a period of two or three months to complete this project, so make sure you have enough time before getting started. Before you begin your project, do some research to find out more about constellations. Once you've done some research, you can tackle this project. Or, you may come up with your own unique project after you've read and learned more about the topic.

Here are some books and websites you could start with in your research:

» Kerrod, Robin. *The Book of Constellations.* New York: Barrons Educational, 2002.

» The Sky Tonight Sky Chart: http://www.skytonight.com/observing/skychart

» Your Sky: http://www.fourmilab.to/yoursky/

Project Information

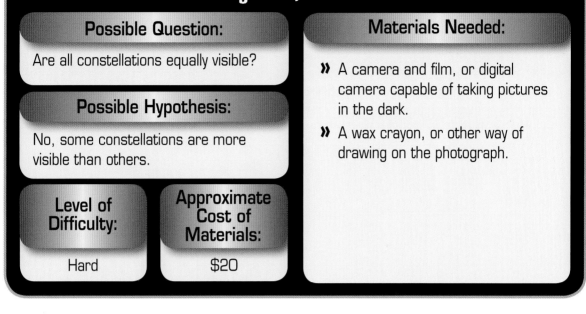

Possible Question:

Are all constellations equally visible?

Possible Hypothesis:

No, some constellations are more visible than others.

Level of Difficulty:

Hard

Approximate Cost of Materials:

$20

Materials Needed:

» A camera and film, or digital camera capable of taking pictures in the dark.

» A wax crayon, or other way of drawing on the photograph.

Steps to Success:

1. Research the constellations that will be visible in your area over the next few months. There are several websites such as http://www.fourmilab.to/yoursky/, that help you locate constellations in your area.

2. Make a plan to find two or more constellations that are supposed to be visible.

Chart

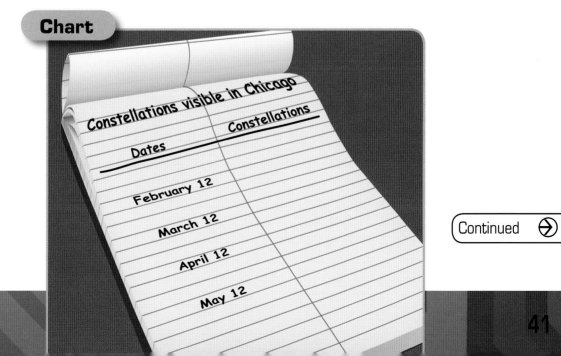

Constellations visible in Chicago

Dates	Constellations
February 12	
March 12	
April 12	
May 12	

Continued →

April 13th

3. On the appropriate night, go outside and see if you can find the constellation. Take a picture of the night sky whether you find the constellation or not. If you live in an area with lots of lights, you may need to ask a trusted adult to drive you to a darker area. It might be helpful to make a sketch of the sky and the constellation as well as taking a photograph.

4. Repeat step 3 for a few nights in a row.

5. Choose a different constellation that will be visible at a different time, perhaps a month later. Repeat steps 2–4.

6. Develop the film, or print the digital pictures, and if possible, mark the constellations on the pictures.

Result Summary:

» Were you able to see both constellations?

» Were you able to see the constellations every night or only on some nights?

» What variables might have affected your ability to see the constellations?

» Can you think of any practical reason for the creation of named constellations?

» Did you notice any other groupings of stars that could be constellations?

Added Activities to Give Your Project Extra Punch:

» If you noticed other groupings of stars, research them to find out if they are named constellations. If they are not consider naming them yourself.

» Have a partner who lives in a different part of your city or town conduct the experiment as well. Compare your notes.

» Find out how constellations were helpful in everyday applications at other times in history.

Display Extras:

» All the pictures you took of the night sky, with dates written on them.

» Art prints of illustrated constellations.

» Pictures of old tools sailors used to navigate by the stars.

The Competition

Learning is it's own reward, but winning the science fair is pretty fun, too. Here are some things to keep in mind if you want to do well in competition:

1) Creativity counts. Do not simply copy an experiment from this or any other book. You need to change the experiment so that it is uniquely your own.

2) You will need to be able to explain your project to the judges. Being able to talk intelligently about your work will help reassure the judges that you learned something, and did the work yourself. You may have to repeat the same information to different judges, so make sure you've practiced it ahead of time. You will also need to be able to answer the judge's questions about your methods and results.

3) You will need to present your materials in an appealing manner. Discuss with your teacher whether or not it is acceptable to have someone help you with artistic flourishes to your display.

Keep these guidelines in mind for your display:

» **Type and print:** Display the project title, the question, the hypothesis, and the collected data in clean, neatly crafted paper printouts that you can mount on a sturdy poster display.

» **Visibility:** Be sure you print your title and headings in large type and in energetic colors. If your project is about the sun, maybe you'll use bright reds, oranges, and yellows to bring your letters to life. If your project is about plant life, maybe you'll use greens and browns to capture an earthy mood. You want your project to be easily visible in a crowd of other projects.

» **Standing display:** Be sure your display can stand on its own. Office supply stores have thick single-, double-, and triple-section display boards available in several sizes and colors that will work nicely as the canvas for your science fair masterpiece. Mount your core data — your discoveries — on this display, along with photos and other relevant materials (charts, resource articles, interviews, etc.).

» **Dress neatly and comfortably for the fair.** You may be standing on your feet for a long time.

4) The final report is an important part of your project.
Make sure the following things are in your final report:

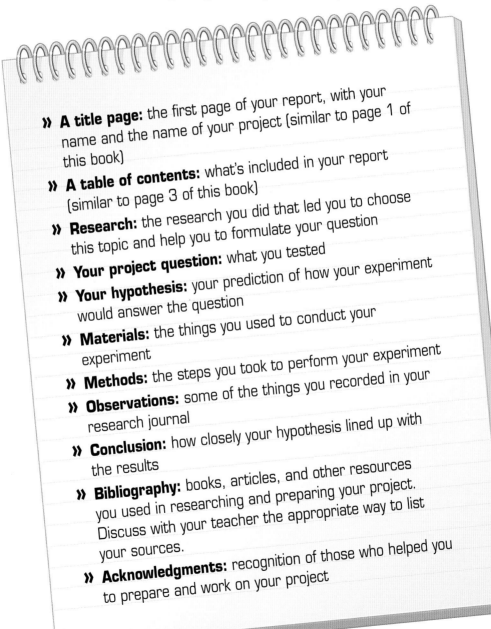

» **A title page:** the first page of your report, with your name and the name of your project (similar to page 1 of this book)

» **A table of contents:** what's included in your report (similar to page 3 of this book)

» **Research:** the research you did that led you to choose this topic and help you to formulate your question

» **Your project question:** what you tested

» **Your hypothesis:** your prediction of how your experiment would answer the question

» **Materials:** the things you used to conduct your experiment

» **Methods:** the steps you took to perform your experiment

» **Observations:** some of the things you recorded in your research journal

» **Conclusion:** how closely your hypothesis lined up with the results

» **Bibliography:** books, articles, and other resources you used in researching and preparing your project. Discuss with your teacher the appropriate way to list your sources.

» **Acknowledgments:** recognition of those who helped you to prepare and work on your project

Prepare to Be Judged

Each science fair is different but you will probably be assigned points based on the categories below. Make sure to talk to your teacher about how your specific science fair will be judged. Ask yourself the questions in each category to see if you've done the best possible job.

Your objectives
» Did you present original, creative ideas?
» Did you state the problem or question clearly?
» Did you define the variables and use controls?
» Did you relate your research to the problem or question?

Your skills
» Do you understand your results?
» Did you do your own work? It's OK for an adult to help you for safety reasons, but not to do the work for you. If you cannot explain the experiment, the equipment, and the steps you took, the judges may not believe you did your own work.

Data collection and interpretation
» Did you keep a research journal?
» Was your experiment planned correctly to collect what you needed?
» Did you correctly interpret your results?
» Could someone else repeat the experiment?
» Are your conclusions based only on the results of your experiment?

Presentation
» Is your display attractive and complete?
» Do you have a complete report?
» Did you use reliable sources and document them correctly?
» Can you answer questions about your work?

Glossary

atmosphere air surrounding Earth

constellation group of stars

control something that is left unchanged in order to compare results against

data information

eclipse complete or partial hiding of an object

ejecta matter that is piled up around a crater

erosion process of breaking down or wearing away

geology/geologist science that studies the history of Earth. Geologists are especially interested in how the history of Earth is recorded in rocks and minerals.

hypothesis unproven assumption based on some evidence

meteorite space matter that reaches Earth

orbit path taken by one object around another object

prediction thought or guess of how something will turn out before it happens

radius line extending from the center of a circle or sphere to the outer edge of the circle or sphere

scientific theory assumption that is not completely proven, but is based on the principles of science

stationary not moving, still

variable element in an experiment that can change

Index